Ethan the Elephant and Friends

Ethan the Elephant's Bath

Ethan the elephant,
he is magnificent,
he has such a long, strong trunk.

He hears a loud squeal,
and sees Evie the Eel
as she circles the water he's drunk.

"What are you doing?
You're draining my pool!"
asked Evie the Eel looking puzzled.
"The water was lovely and clean and so cool,
but there's none left now that you have guzzled!"

"Please don't worry, I'll have your water back in a hurry!"
said Ethan the Elephant with a laugh.
"Even though it looks yummy, it's not in my tummy,
I was using it for a nice bath!"

Ethan raises his trunk and aims high in the air,
then squirts out water with such speed and power.
Evie giggles, as she races and wiggles,
"Instead of a bath it's a shower!"

Fiona Flamingo's Rescue Mission

Fiona Flamingo dances on the beach
and suddenly hears a hollering screech.
She looks up above and what does she see?
It's Freddy the Ferret, he's stuck up a tree!

"Please help me down, I'm right at the top.
I got over excited and did a big backward hop,
then landed up high on top of these leaves.
Oh help me down Fiona, please!"

"I'm far too high up to try and jump,
as it's such a long way to the ground.
If you don't save me soon I might land with a bump,
should I slip off these leaves and fall down."

Fiona Flamingo says "Help is at hand!"
and leaps off her one standing leg from the sand.
Once up in the air, she then starts to fly,
and rescues Freddy the Ferret from up high in the sky.

"Thank you Fiona Flamingo!" he says,
as they both touch back down to the ground.
"The next time I promise to be more careful,
so that I'll remain safe and sound."

Gary Gorilla's Treat

Let's eat some ice cream with Gary Gorilla .
He loves it so much , his favourite's vanilla.
He's been such a good ape that he deserves a nice treat,
and he really likes ice cream because it's so sweet!

Grace the Giraffe is eating leaf flavoured jelly.
It slides down her long neck and into her belly.

Grace the Giraffe tries to pick up her bowl,
but drops it right onto the floor.
She looks down at her feet, and sees her spilled treat,
Grace won't eat leaf jelly anymore.

Gary sees the spilled jelly and this makes him feel bad.
He does not want to see poor Grace feeling sad,
so to show her just how much that he really cares,
he takes half of his ice cream and leans over and shares!

Gary's kind sharing makes Grace feel much better,
as the friends finish off their nice treats together.

Henrik the Horse's Shopping Trip

We love him of course, it's Henrik the Horse
and he won't be stopping , on his way to go shopping.
As he hurriedly moves, the sound of his hooves
go 'clip clip a clopping', he's grooving and bopping!

He passes Harry Hedgehog on the way
to buy himself a nice big stack of hay.
Henrik the Horse, he gallops with force
and Trots off to do his shopping.

Harry Hedgehog, he sleeps like a log
and he'll doze all day, by the street cafe.
Be careful not to wake him, please don't disturb him
with a whinny, a neigh , or a loud 'hip horaay'!

Harry's covered in spines which are sturdy and fine
and they'll keep him warm and snug when he wakes up at night.
Harry Hedgehog, he sleeps like a log
and he'll sleep all day , as Henrik eats his hay.

Ignacio Iguana's Fun in the Sun

You can find him in the treetops,
basking in the sun .
Sprawled out on a large branch ,
he's having lots of fun!

Feasting on a mango,
turnip greens and a banana,
he loves his fruit and vegetables,
he's Ignacio Iguana .

His long scaly body rises
as he starts to rush and dash,
and he dives into the water
where he makes a giant splash!

From the Caribbean Islands
to Brazil and Mexico,
a lovely green Iguana swims,
his name's Ignacio.

E e

F f

G g

H h

I i

Using water saving techniques, like Ethan the Elephant does, diverts less water from our rivers, which helps keep the environment healthy.

If climbing a tree, don't go too high, as there may not be a Flamingo close by to help you back down!

Jelly and ice cream
are delicious treats
and great to have
occasionally at parties
or for a special reward
for doing great at school.

Hedgehogs are nocturnal animals,
meaning they're active during the night
and sleep during daylight hours.

Iguanas are native to
Central America,
South America
and the Caribbean Islands.

Part of the
Ava the Anteater and Friends
series of rhyming stories

With all my love to Michael, Mia, Esme
and Rosa.

Text and illustration copyright © Beth
Tamwell
ISBN 978 1 9989976 0 2

Published by: Beth Tamwell
bethtamwell@yahoo.com

www.ingramcontent.com/pod-product-compliance
Lightning Source LLC
Chambersburg PA
CBHW041529120626
46551CB00018B/2624